The Slowing Ride

ALSO BY WILL STONE

POETRY
Glaciation Shearsman Books (2015; 1st edition, Salt Publishing, 2007)
Drawing in Ash Shearsman Books (2015; 1st edition, Salt Publishing, 2011)
The Sleepwalkers Shearsman Books (2016)

TRANSLATIONS
Les Chimères – Gérard de Nerval Shearsman Books (2018; 1st edition,
        Menard Press 1999)
Poems – Emile Verhaeren Arc Publications (2013)
Montaigne – Stefan Zweig Pushkin Press (2015)
Messages from a Lost World – Stefan Zweig Pushkin Press (2016)
Poems – Georges Rodenbach Arc Publications (2017)
Journeys – Stefan Zweig Pushkin Press (2019; 1st edition, Hesperus
        Press, 2010)
Rilke in Paris – Rainer Maria Rilke & Maurice Betz Pushkin Press
        (2019; 1st edition, Hesperus Press, 2012)
On the End of the World – Joseph Roth Pushkin Press (2019;
        1st edition, Hesperus Press, 2013)
Surrender to Night – *Collected Poems of Georg Trakl* Pushkin Press (2019)
Nietzsche – Stefan Zweig Pushkin Press (2020; 1st edition, Hesperus
        Press, 2013)
Encounters and Destinies, A Farewell to Europe – Stefan Zweig Pushkin
        Press (2020)
Poems to Night – Rainer Maria Rilke Pushkin Press (2020)

Will Stone

The
Slowing
Ride

Shearsman Books

First published in the United Kingdom in 2020 by
Shearsman Books Ltd
PO Box 4239
Swindon
SN3 9FN

Shearsman Books Ltd Registered Office
30–31 St. James Place, Mangotsfield, Bristol BS16 9JB
(this address not for correspondence)

www.shearsman.com

ISBN 978-1-84861-716-2

For my parents

My starting point has to be a vision…

Jakob Burckhardt

Contents

III

Contents

III

I

One can belong to a people but when the people fall prey to insanity one is not obliged to remain in the same time as them.

Stefan Zweig

Song of the West

It is a spring rain come at last
and the white doves will not leave the tower.
Aware, the tree crowns sway, take what is owed.
The grey green sea where later a sail might show,
plumage down which the rain beads gently go
losing themselves, but each remains a gemstone.
In the wood there is a torn quilt of silence
and with reluctance the old priory walls
have recalled their long shadows.
The bay is a deep cave where eyes wait
and the drift of smoke and bells sinks down.
The stranger passed behind leaded lights
in the weft of forebodings, he stayed on
as another's fingers ran like frightened deer
across the keys, with pure instinct
then suddenly slowed, in time
each creature senses our downfall.

Latecomers

In clover fields, flax, or barley still green
a mist of fallow deer, far off, afraid.
Our approach brought love, but they turned
and as one moved away.
A yearning for islands, fruit-stocked shorelines
imagined through eyes closing with salt.

Nature, the patient persistent labourer
who does not look up as we pass.
Here, where the insane rose from holes
like heaven denied souls, and minions at web centre
wove their black silk, the impossible perfected
through stray nightingale song or prayer,
the same trunks are thicker in the grove.
There the old Ruthenian with glittering eyes
lent a smile to the child who never saw,
so absorbed plaiting weed flowers and grasses.
I watched them descend the slope with care
to lower their little cans into the bitter ditch.
Then the dust rose in that waiting place
and the breeze gently removed their spaces.

Overconfidently light returns to the summit
following the storm. The shepherd darkness.
We descend now to the valley in shadow,
a few finding tree crowns and the amber eyes
of forest animals, streams rolling with sun.
The rest are found later, trussed with frost,
their eyes become mother of pearl.

After the Storm

Moon, spectre beyond daybreak,
resting on the oak's invalid crown.
Through any crack seeps history
and we now at the storm's edge,
beginners in our nest till we fly or fall,
today, tomorrow or further on,
ending high or broken on the road.
In whose light are we saved, sun or moon?
Sound of burnt angels drifting down,
reeds of Iken moving as one.
Or we retire under the soft weave
of a nun's hands in the lily heavy room,
the sister who knelt before her saviour's
greening desert tree and for beauty
sang in the high cathedral of Sion.
Now the white wayfarer is in retreat,
a strengthening sun sends out riders,
heirlooms this generation will accept,
but the tomb inscription of a noble line
can no longer be detected.

The Last Pilot

On Memorial Day he stares out
to the channel that overlooked him,
saw brothers then who raised fist or thumb
from the lonely trail into swell and chasm.
He the last of them now, the remaining bricks
of the wall long crumbled back to sand.
They were directed towards the directed,
racing over chatter and human derangement
Well we had to stop them at any cost
they wanted to enslave us…
It was a hard thing when a chum disappeared.
All gone elsewhere now, the squadron disbanded.
From straw-filled Nissen huts come swallows,
saplings rudely crowd the trimmed pathways
and greedily the wind works at the glass,
the last clear fragment that clings to the frame.
Voices deleting each time you look up,
another consumed star leaves a space.
But darkness shrank back and on each casket
was laid the weightless wreath of light.

Death of a Trophy Hunter

Over the kill the larvae loom
she posted on Instagram
before the blood congealed,
paid in dollars for the fun.
Trophy hunter with a smile
herself hunted down on the net,
they published her name, address.
Not overheated reaction, not revenge
not justice even, the vigilantes said
only the necessary removal of a stain.
By the noble king's massive head
she makes the thumbs up sign,
ajar the jaw in spasm, from within
came once the ancient roar,
final tearing of a tree's roots
blow of power you felt quiver
through the enclosure's rock wall.
She walks away from the corpse,
prepares to update her webpage.
They wait her followers, the last men,
itching to share conspiratorially,
as the beams of lighthouses sweep
for faith in the infinite darkness.

Goya

By the end he was deaf
but he still heard
the laughter of the insane,
a human claw against the pane
and the scrape of nails
around the asylum wall.
He watched the old witch
bite down on a babe's downy thigh
and saw rough peasants cross the sky
figures falling half-naked
in dispute, in embrace.

Each page, a pale craft gradually passed
through his narrow canal of ink.

Everything outside shook him
but only insight fell out.
He moved away from men
forced a passage, his dark prow
broke the ice into bright backgrounds
on which the lonely were placed.
Goya, he forced back the eyelid
of the unseeing, then got out
before it closed again for good.

The Bones of Faith

Ice wall at the end of the world.
Trapped there are the explorers,
with blunted bow, tethered like dogs
to the confused mission of the floes.
Their convictions placed in shrouds
slip into the dark waters of the sound.
On deck they line up in their furs
before the ice cliff arisen from nowhere
with confidence, the unexplained
that overhung the strongest human child.
Memories are all the pioneers have,
flapping weakly in cages on the deck.
The gold in the chest shines uselessly,
how easily insanity found their location.
Each held a flame to the blue grey whiteness
but what came back was a darkness, then
distance worked its knife into them.
The sun rose and possibility of survival
shared amongst them its gaudy promises.
In frost-caked corners and by waning stoves
they lay stacked like wood piles in snow.
Some prayed, called for Lord Jesus Christ,
but on the last day there was only the ice.
Then silence slipped on board, a grey fox,
to snatch the last reserves of words.

Stolen Girls

I came upon them in London drifting,
survivors from a wreck consumed by dark seas.
Behind them looms the last crime, in front
the future hones another charismatic psychopath
or a free thinker bent over his lathe, alone.
Stolen girls, robbed before their ripening,
lost in the guarded emporiums through which
they briefly assuage their emptiness, drawn back
like the lonely nun to the saint's posy of bones.
Melancholy hovers over them, all is movement
but still as Tuileries statues darkening in rain.
At memorials for others their own wreath is laid,
for their miraculous origin is now a buried relic
passed over, peered at behind security glass,
in whose reflection the unseeing appear and fade.
The powerful thieves of their purity proceed,
shadows of late men and plausible explanations
behind cruel pub windows of black ice.

The Slowing Ride

Higher they rose on the Ferris wheel
in their cold nest that creaked.
The sun found them at 12 o'clock
when the ride slowed and stopped.
Warm now were closed lids and lips,
her hair wild with cries on the way up
lay silent, a beautiful weary creature.
The world below could not reach them,
its shadows moved stiffly beneath ice.
They held hands as if before a crash
and waited, suspended over the crater.
Suddenly two childhoods, strangers
rose to join them, seraphs on the scent
of new mown grass, the ochre perfume
of giant leaf piles, they fell back into.
Laughing, they burst out of the willow,
ran through glittering ropes from a hose.
It was summer and time could not reply.
He ran into the woods, was not followed.
The slender tree swayed with his weight
but the branches held, and strongly he rose,
to the hiding place, where he was safe
on the hill they called Drummer's Maid.
Then the great wheel began to turn.
A wolf pack turned towards the sun,
they felt the quickening thaw,
dark hungry forms moved upwards,
as too violently the car clattered in.
They hauled them out the silent strays,
two more leapt into their warmth,
laughing, shrieking, hoisted up
through the settling cinders.

Rarae Avis

In the Hunterian Museum, The Royal College of Surgeons, London.

Suspended in formaldehyde
as if on hooks, six infant foetuses
snatched in record time by science.
Umbilicals like unearthed roots drift
searching vainly for new soil,
milky vapour trails in the ether.
Furious these century old celebrities,
with dark frowns and clenched fists
for they were wrenched from death,
forced to stare out at the living who pass,
forever left to inhabit their own wreck.
Ghoulish is their frantic puppetry,
so needlessly tight the thimble fists
and their mouths a petulant slit
and their arms like a dog's toy bone
frozen in some chance gesticulation,
a first gesture of greeting abandoned.
These pale monkeys obey their fate
joining what is unidentified in space.
Girl voyeurs gaze through the glass,
they grin, grimace, point a finger,
then letting out theatrical screams
run out into the sun's spreading arms
to flashing eyes and warm forms
away from the bloodless ruins.

The Madwoman at Gloucester Road

From the top deck of the 74 bus,
the icy laughter of mischievous gods.
In the misted pane she draws a face
tunneling her way out to further mischief,
to darken one of the million lit windows
where the chosen ones sensually slip
from lush shiraz into evening dress.
Then she stabs bellows at the trapped,
her whirlwind is black as the storm speech
that orders the fishing boats into the harbour.
For only *her* voice must reign, racing in
to meet the dead ends, the boom of a wave
in the lonely cove where no one comes.
Then like the sudden squall she is gone.
As we pull away I look down, see her
bent back, one arm raised in defiance,
like a weed choked figurehead winched
up from the depths, a question mark
hanging over the ocean.

Lip Service

It was a funeral. We were alive.
Hearses kept coming down the drive,
slowly, deliberately, unendingly,
like gleaming pampered race horses
led one by one from the paddock.
The crematorium had ample parking,
the priest had notes, some underlined
but she dramatically misread the name
and poem titles of the good European,
the Belgian poet to whom the deceased
had dedicated a biography and her life.
I wanted to take to task this woman of God,
who had gruesomely dispatched Verhaeren.
But after a token appearance at the wake
the priest gathered up her cassock
heaved herself into a sports utility vehicle
and drove off at speed with her holy wafers.

Port Town in December

At dusk the lights of the port appear
and coloured bulbs strung on black wires
jig hopefully above the promenade.
The grubby surf turns, with a pout
lays before us its morbid subsistence.
Battered hulls and torn sails litter
the lacklustre beachside café.
From here they watch the old pier
stagger naked into the gloom.
In the long abandoned theatre
wind and wave sound wrestle
amongst the litter of the last act,
grim farewells, the rind of lost activity,
a dried out encore flattened in a trap.
And a black dog is in the breakers
cigarette thrown, streak of cinders.
A landslide of crows onto the road
then half-lifting off with carcass load.
The wound we saved and took home.

The Guiltless

This was their last chance
search for an escape route out,
last rag wound round the torch.
Over bare dunes the cortege passed,
over mountains strung with vines,
over mist terraces of birch forests
where lay gentle Russian princesses
identified by jewel-armoured bodices,
inscribed prayer books left behind.
Bergs break off and move out to sea,
the great migration of geese has begun,
running herds all brown plunge into gullies
chests against the power of blue estuaries.
Nature the one God has no need for angels.
Marguerite Bervoets, Belgian heroine
walks calmly from her cell to the block,
through the black curtains to martyrdom.
Luggage left on a ramp outlined by snow,
red hood of the boy receding, mother
her vague form sharpened a moment
by the forge glow of upward sparks.
Always the guiltless set out their stall,
each word chosen leaves a fresh wound.
They will make safe with ash
the ice path of the unborn.

II

When all buildings are destroyed, language will nevertheless persist. It will be an enchanted castle with towers and battlements, with primeval vaults and passages which none will ever search out. There in deep galleries, oubliettes and mine-shafts one will be able to find habitation and be lost from the world. At this hour such a thought consoles me.

Ernst Jünger
Paris Journals, 1943

Possession of the Florentine

Lines written in the old priory cottage, Dunster, March 2020

So it passes the desiring eye
passes over locked coffer
cassapanca or cassone,
Florentine ivory comb
once owned by the loved one
or the cruelly deceived,
who felt the foliage of orange trees
the cherub's levelled arrow,
daily read the braille of beauty
the artist's landscape emerging
from early mists giving way to the sun.
All that has come down to us
but moving away now behind glass,
the delicate clavier of broken teeth
whose every key plays faultlessly.
Through morning tresses they sang
and in the evening again, at Vespers
the soft tread on darkening grass
the flock returning home.
Raised and lowered, turned to the light
like an unearthed gemstone
those scenes and myths he chose
her tender fingers kindled,
until the moment raised swords
rattled on walls in the narrow stairwell,
three centuries enshrouded
then the traveller emerged into light
and with buds unknowingly bloomed.
Laid like a new born on black velvet
each polished tooth eager to harrow

the scented soil as then,
but the future is for sculpture alone,
preservation, existence without air,
before the gaze of the uncomprehending
the envious, the lost, what has amassed
before the sun in its decline,
though each day it rises
our shattering impermanence.

The Final Journey

Shaded square of chestnuts in autumn
one by one heavily dropped the husks
from windows in the Karmeliterplatz.
Roman pool, there you could float or drown,
but Diana pool was out of bounds.
The old park showed no recognition.
chairs stacked, carrousel stopped, kiosk closed
and new masters on the sinuous pathway.
Each night they saw the torch glow on walls
saw those they had known cup their hands
under the dripping fang of the mad dog.
They felt the massive volt of destruction,
heard of new fiefdoms where out of forges
hate's edge was hammered, perfected.
The fathers bore their anguish alone,
noble faces passed from pane to pane
in courtyards children laughed unknowing,
the old called down to them lovingly
and listless doves patrolled the eaves.
Briefcases freshly fattened sat in the aisles,
the architects were borne on gleaming rails,
eyes of different colours for monochrome
and a train whistle, long and cold.
With the lists of names in purple ink,
they burst through the ring of firs.

Two Poems After Trakl

De Profundis

There is a pine forest on which an acid rain falls.
There is a tree of limbs that stands lonely here.
There is a nuclear wind that haunts abandoned new homes –
How criminal this century.

Past the darkening suburb
the dazed runaway still begs from a sleeping bag.
Red and pinched her eyes burn in the headlights
and her swollen womb awaits the backstreet quack.

Returning home
night watchmen found the surplus body
stiffened in a cardboard box.

A player, I am remote from sepulchral towers.
The anthrax of amen
I licked from the weeping wall.

On my brow mad lasers play.
Science seeks my heart.
There is a tongue in my mouth which is cut.

At night I found myself upon a runway
thick with screams and siren blasts.
Beneath the groaning bridge
brown rats have feasted once more.

Grodek

At nightfall the suburbs incubate
with stealthy disease and welling rage,
the pale cul-de-sacs, above which more darkly
carves the moon, the night by-passes
bereaved women, the muffled scream
of their inoperable hearts.
But quietly there in the playground
forgotten childhood where no greed resides,
tears shed evaporate, ocean unconcerned.
Under stars unseen for the sodium glow
the reaper rides the empty ring road,
to greet the ghosts passed on by tactful undertakers;
and softly the horn of future sounds
through the swaying jibs of dockyard cranes.
Oh unimpeded cycle! You boarded up altars,
today a terrible affliction upsets the inspired signal,
the womb blind yet unborn.

Rooks

Under burial skies, over lonely copses
in their greasy mourning wear,
they push inland from the wild east.
They march past snow-bound farmsteads,
where thick black smoke rises and hens
jerk blindly over hard bare earth.
Finally they reach the desired field
to ride the Ferris wheel of themselves,
peeling off the summit on serrated wing
to shred again the sky's dark clothing.
Over waves of frozen hawthorn
and the ice armour of ponds
their shining bead eyes spill.

Celan in Stuttgart

On the 250th anniversary of the birth
of the poet Friedrich Hölderlin

Without a willow frond, with reticence
came the poet to Stuttgart fifty years ago.
Summoned for the reciting of poems
before the ranks of learned burghers,
two hundred years since the cradle cry
of one too fragile, who broke.
At the lectern he appeared and read,
branches moving across glass
some tiny mammal in a hole of grass
appeared hopefully, then backed away.
Terrible voices forced a way through stone,
nothing he read was published or known
nothing referred to the one celebrated.
Sometimes this genius goes dark
and sinks down into the bitter well
of his heart.
Two months later, Paris.
In hostile landscape a running prey
distanced himself from the hunters,
slipped through snow-weighted firs,
only the furthest stars lent their light
to record a passing shadow
upon the scree of firn.

Debris Field

High anxiety of world calamity,
in soiled shop doorways the silenced
emerge to beg from cardboard boxes.
Breezes stir the ashen peaks of the forest,
the trees bend their purity altogether
before the lake's dark mirror.
The tyrant again secures safe passage.
Jawbone of a fox white in the fir forest,
bark dust in a web, blade of a torrent.
In a clearing red deer ringed by darkness,
bramble now invades the secret path
gentle monks may once have taken.
The sand track is skeletal and cold,
it leads to reactor or crematoria.
From the copse of silver birches
the procession of lepers is coming,
frost around the mouth of their bells.

Three Days

At party conference
I saw skulls –
neat rows and pyramids as at Kutna Hora
or the catacombs below Denfert Rochereau.
Cadavers of ideas were wheeled in to applause
by asylum orderlies in scarlet tunics.
Fat media crows hopped at the entrances
and happy dogs leapt on stage
to be fondled and patted, though none
could be coerced to drop the severed limb.

I was walking down the road with two friends
when the sun set; suddenly, the sky turned red as blood...
I felt a terrible scream pass through nature.

Hospitals, prisons, tax breaks, law and order,
a joke drops like a suicide from the Chancellor
then lesser mannequins at the rostrum
badly painted and poorly strung.
The governing hand finally fails,
becomes a sideways scooping palm.
The auditorium empties, the bars roar.
Bulldozers with their shining grins
sweep the remains into
carefully prepared excavations.

Charenton

In memoriam Charles Meryon, etcher of Paris (1821-1868)

When the sun left its blood pool
at the back of the black wood,
his dirty carriage drew up to the asylum.
The directors or deceiving lunatics
formed a line and curtly bowed,
for the emperor had arrived.
Welcome to Charenton, a tall man creaked
like a dead elm in the wind.
The dwarf burst forth to take the bags,
the portfolio he would not relinquish.
The linen was fresh and neatly piled,
horribly aligned the brush and comb.
In the dead black water of the pail
his alien planetary face emerged.
Despite their reassurances
the smock of paper and leaves
provided little warmth,
and the clogs were hard as hazel shells.
To sleep standing up strapped to a board
was not encouraged here.
A man dressed as a doctor looked him over,
the mouth opened like a fish behind glass
but he heard only the blackbirds
fussing in the bushes at dusk.
He was soon engaged on menial tasks,
then sent to the vegetable gardens
with a basket to bring back
stinking onions, the severed heads.
At night he burrowed into the soft earth
of his maritime voyages.

Dawn's gaining light softened the bars,
pale pink ribbon bows blooming
out of the dark hair of girls,
those to whom he had wildly proposed,
then watched their dark capes sink
like ashes in the stairwell.
Alone, he dug for treasure in the yard
and here he was found, haranguing the sky
amidst unidentified bones.

The Shoot

When stubble fields are blackened
with birds bred for destruction,
before the beater makes one eye vast,
body a strung bow, then the plunge
into bloody down and smoke, half-lid
closed by the breath of a hound.

Jewish children in Polish meadows
plaiting daisies while they wait,
cannot return with their last seconds
to show us, cupped in a palm.
Here beneath the German ocean,
bells of a lost city wait beneath silt,
from weakened cliff a skull emerges.

Crows

In winter winds the crows fly so strongly,
land so gently on the dead oak's crown,
like a black-gloved hand on a lifeless brow.
Uppermost branches are their rigging
climbing silvery grey, taut or bowing
and all the calling is gathered there,
formed and re-formed, each wheeling cry
a lazy rope, thrown to arcane signs.
Those below who may watch them
performing their dark ministrations
point knowingly but do not understand.
Bickering, these captains on the bridge
seem as if still commanding, in control,
but their young sway silently in baskets
beneath them, untaught, lonely,
new explorers without history
who never return.

Last Rose

After a photograph by Josef Sudek

Last rose born cold
sad as a litter-less pig's eye,
last makeshift raft of colour
adrift on the dark tarn of ivy.
Rose of autumn the scouts
of the first frosts condemned,
casually daubed with a cross,
like our relatives in rest homes
who do not return. But elsewhere
light is gaining, sun and birdsong
frolic like oblivious infants, shadows
lie like the weary Antwerp tiger
by the plunge pool, he who succumbed
and was winched out in light rain
above the bristling copse of cameras.
Hawkers of new dawns, humankind
with a retinue of signalling centuries,
kneel and place your new old stone
upon the slow-built cairn of history
and crowded into your wagons of love
enter the territory of desolation.

Blood Fridge

Crows thrown back inland by gusts,
stubble field with swallows low at dusk,
those seen fairies stitch with silver thread
the landscape's freshest wounds.
Deep pain goes unrecorded.
Those who loved and held each other
wait patiently by the blood fridge.
Grim jokes, those dark mice scamper
between the stoic elderly people.
Frozen fingers push through wire,
crusts or a message fall in the mud,
even a single wave can be enough
to let a heart couple with the sun.
Now the first winds of autumn come,
dark strangers burst into my garden.
The last apples, those that hung on
unknowing of spring's miracle
drop obediently to the earth.

Lair

The crowd wolfs its meat before the podium,
since horrifying insects have hatched again,
their new old machinery works so impressively
blindfolded women still warm in fur coats
may be calmly led through the dusking wood.
One more time there will be no paper trail,
only a billion shared images.

III

We are members of a world, which, producing movement upon movement, force upon force, seems to be plunging irresistibly into a less visible state and we are dependent on that superior visibility of the past if we wish to present an image of the mutual splendour that surrounds us.

Rainer Maria Rilke

Vanished Spirit of Bruges

For Anette Van de Wiele

Old courtyards, chapels and hospices
footfalls muted, carapaces of devotion
and soft singing of the mad woman
behind the grille, a yellowed Christ
laid out on a long ship of candles.
Behind the dark tree of the Jew's altar
the whispers of beguines, deceased piety
as onto the warm dome of the abbey
the carillon sweeps its grey snow,
lonely as venetian glass behind which
no living face has passed all winter,
lonely as velvet which accepts the ring,
lonely as lime leaves on the black canal
lonely as the swan, the air's ferryman,
lonely as inaudible past atmospheres
still signalling from the flames.

The Garden of Silence

Following a visit to the Monastery island of St Giulio, Orta.

Forbidden enclosure, steeply rising
whose worn stone and dying paths
conspire to drink the shade alone.
Convent garden denying the unblessed,
passage blocked to the lush sanctum
by iron gates always firmly locked,
eternally secure, never breached.
Only finger width gaps where it dwells
the thirsting eye of the solitary.
Narrow gaps and a few chance holes
the honed enchantment leaks through,
glut of scents, above the crowd
drones bred to press in, lay siege
to the last desperate flowering.
Come twilight there are stirrings,
nuns flit suddenly over toy bridges
cleverly screened with trellis and vines,
ensuring no-one collects by eye or lens
proof of these rare moths, shadows of doves
trapped in a basilica, back and forth
light then dark, the pain of predicament,
dwindling shoals exploring defiance
and danger, in honour of the anchorite.
You gaze up the spirals of stone steps,
past infant ferns to the tiny sacred peak,
guarded by gently determined fruit.
Over you pass the shades of the dead
with their train of under-leaf darkness,
that stillness they crave is found here
in what is concealed, closed in, muted,

refuge from the disease within a crowd,
from the boundless heat-quivering plain
with its dark serpent of flagellants.

The Jackdaw's Gift

The jackdaws have flown,
they left no forwarding address.
We took their home for kindling
out of the chimney stack, the whole nest,
twig halos from many trees,
tiny tumbleweeds, mossy bark medallions.
Each day they brought a little more,
rising higher, thickening under the stars.
Here brigand chieftains patrolled,
their self-praise clunking over the tiles.
Each evening the grate lapped up all they built,
each day flames crash through
the clan's arduous labour spent,
like the unseen wave over Embelle's shore,
that carried the completed driftwood in, only there
from the retreating sculptor's form.
No reply, only scrub oaks and gulls,
stray lamb amidst a woodland's broken bones.
The rooftops of a medieval village
darken together in the rain
and our fire sensing the shift of logs
strains at the end of its taut chain.

High Tide at Porlock Weir

For Margaret Holroyd

The silent hunter has returned,
the little boats sleep on.
Along the creek her predatory form
uncoils darkly beneath the arch.
She nudges forward the sailboats,
but with anchors stern and aft
they are leashed, unable to advance.
With her swag of momentum,
she overwhelms again the old stones
with their vines of rusting chain,
fleecing the shale, ignoring the cries
of fat crows that hop at her side.
Over marsh grass and the grey bones
of a skiff, her currents consolidate.
She eyes her prey, the shore path,
slips on new land like an evening gown.
But all she stole must be left behind,
as above the oak, a new moon
bright echo of an earlier beauty,
signals her dominion is at an end.
She retreats, but never in disarray,
the paths glisten with awakening,
hulls whisper as she passes.

Gentle Travellers

When dusk commits, pauses
on the edge of night's plantation,
when the crescent moon rests her toe
on the summit of the copse, then
their tiny cries rise from the ivy,
dark ones looping the elms, the ash.

Tintabula or carillon, petals of iron
swept out of the day, the bats
they are whispering over our eyes,
turning velvet current into signs
silken thread into secretive mime.
These strangers who say trespasser
flicker-meet your gaze, you follow, in vain
dull rock in the spray, groping day dweller.

Everything for them is circumference,
their task completed ahead of the dance.
Every wing grazing your face is a wish,
every arc, every spiral a slow persuasion.
Down rescued from the long dead bird
their touch, ash that settles, rises and you
left holding the melting wire of their act.

Sweffling

For Anne Beresford

Summer evening
in the churchyard of Sweffling,
the sound carrousel is still turning.
Indolent perfumes of meadow flowers,
buttercups half-open, unable to close,
a moth caught on a web finally fails.
Behind the foaming hawthorn crest,
the sun stretches a beam arm out
into darkening foliage and climbers
that hoard the old brick wall.
Distant voices, a cross of wood decayed
falls back into the arms of nettles,
loved like the disabled crab apple
or the iron gates leading nowhere.
Suddenly it grows colder, the blackbird
stops dead on a dark yew branch.
Norman arch and names in stone
long effaced, their ardent signatures
the leggy rosemary has smothered.
Down through lichened tombs
goes the herald in retirement,
stone angel with severed wing.

Starlings Bathing

In a bare winter field made up of men
downwind of the Thiepval memorial,
they descend in gangs to blacken
February's furrow pools of pearl and milk.
Hundreds; lifting, dropping, veering
pestering, preening, plashing, bathing
in feathery electricity and helpless beauty.
Yet it was here the shire boys stepped out,
calves tethered downwind of the whistle,
obeying the cane and unholstered pistol
with the heat of the rum on their throat,
swiftly they slipped into prepared shafts.
Militarized herds were reared to be loved
but they left like the horses, ripped apart,
so oncoming thinkers, researchers, scholars
might sift and sort whatever remains,
handle more gently speeches, assurances,
the scattered porcelain limbs of dolls.
Now the bathers towel down in the breeze,
restored they rise in delirious spirals
directly into the sun, shedding darkness,
cleaned of the blood.

The Bunkers at Wissant

Once they were masters of the horizon,
the steel of their blast doors shone,
the barrels in their clean mouths moved
confidently side to side, up and down.
Loyal minions fussed around them,
made ready their metal honeycomb.
Like leashed dogs they lay in wait,
through storms or on clear starry nights
when a low moon kissed their bald crowns.
But the invasion passed around them,
guns torn out, they were abandoned.
Hollow and silent, they remained rooted
like trees condemned with a cross.
Resignedly they rebranded themselves
as lavatories, a mortuary for tramps.
Then they began to sink, pitch forward,
livestock drawn to drink the mere waters
through their half-moon embrasures.
Partially submerged, as if in limbo
they are unable to retreat or move on.
Old men fish beside their senile forms,
on their grey hide in white paint
'Baignade Interdite', but in summer
swimmers lay their towels there,
to steam on the baking concrete.

Descent from Exmoor

Spine of hills purple with heather,
young ferns that quiver without you
in the ceaseless moorland wind.
The wind turns sheep's wool on wire,
silver grass makes way for the deer,
only the old stones that sense a palm,
are worthy to forge a pact with time.
In the cottage of Coleridge they stare
at miniature sheaves of the poet's hair
changing black to white like all the rest,
a mourning broach given after death.
Not yet corrupted, beautiful children
offer you their trust and feeble half fist,
the warm tears on their ruddy faces
graft themselves onto your passing hand.
On the moor alone you encounter
an immense sadness, but also a hope,
the lost black lamb you must carry back
down the combe of charcoal burners,
through the steep wood of sessile oak
above the sea's fanatical existence.

The Gore

Where Exmoor slips into the sea
below lowered swords of streams,
before Worthy, Yearnor and Culbone,
she descends to the bathhouse at dawn.
On the sickle of the gore I see her form
against the dark smuggler's arch,
hesitation before soft grey vermilion.
Her steps have subsided by the lookout,
where the philosopher's view is masked
by foliage and the little lantern hangs dead.
What's left, when the search is called off?
Driftwood on a shale ridge, placed by surf
at night like the mysterious gift of a cat,
the sea-cleaned white skeleton of a fox.
Breeze in the young fragrant bracken,
rotting boughs that spill from the cliff
your hand hopeful torchlight on walls,
but what's ended dissolves at your touch.
Then a toe hold, a quick sinking pail
your body winched up its youth.
Here a tracing of the old path…
Silk of legend flows through holly and elms
lowering her from the little tower,
secret escape that now leads nowhere,
only into the gull's quivering shift
the landslide's brutal face.

The White Moor

Gripping nature's golden key
and breathing to a built in obeisance,
like pack mules we ascend the old road
where the fanatics cannot go,
the dread men of conviction,
for their acid burns nothing here,
their wild foreground gestures fade.

A celebration of some kind,
crowds line the lane, beeches
atop hard mud banks swept
by the squall of leafage and rain.
We are on our way to the white moor,
where heather posies and yellow grasses
lap around the black bergs of ponies.

Loneliness loved and the little church
held nobly in the fold, the sudden punch
of a farm dog at the limit of a chain,
head rising out of the swell, gone again.
Foals circle the mother's barrel of blood,
turning, tracing, their huge dark eyes
a treasure whose origin is never located.

A solitary rider passes unnoticed
signalling to the shy opening of ferns.

Lost Domain

In Worthy Wood near Culbone
the sun peers through scrub oaks,
haunted sycamore, dead elms.
This lonely path by the laurel,
to serpentine brick tunnels
choked with briar and holly,
these severed follies, anchored
yet marooned, harbouring
last gestures of lepers
the ground mist of their bells.
Terraces descending to the sea
carved out for poets, mathematicians,
aristocrats, order and art
ripped apart by brutal growth
of unchecked bay and rhododendrons.
Vial of opium left on a lichened ledge,
her pale face in the wake of chimera
leaves its wash on the final sketch
of the lady walk. Only an outline
within the dark frame of subsidence,
the bones of the frustrated washed
by weather to a purity beyond silence.
They say there are ghosts, they say
candle flames emerge at night
around this sarcophagus.

Airborne

In memory of Rosamond Richardson (1945–2017)

Encounter with glass.
I lifted the broken without experience,
settled him on a bier of dried grass.
That strange weightlessness, curiosity
after the calm stride of horror,
the miniscule warmth still there,
telling blood bead for an eye.
I drew open the slow-created wing
but it drew back, as if unable to bear
the final gesture of the mechanism.
So here was proof, the secret design
sudden death had missed, the moment
like a first tear halted on a cheek.
Little pulse you were on your way,
then a trap was sprung, a jaw closed
nimbus moved over the sun.
This year's barley crop will carry on,
but you lay there inert on my palm
as our cortege waits at the field edge.
I bid farewell in the whirl of insects,
amidst the slow dragging of bees
dusted with pollen, faint but resilient
I hear your stillborn song.

Notes on the Poems

I

After the Storm

The cathedral of Sion is situated in the Valais region of Switzerland whose artery is the river Rhone. Sited on a rocky hill above the largely preserved old town the church and surrounds were a favourite destination for the poet Rilke, when during his final years he resided in the medieval tower of Muzot in the foothills above Sierre, some twenty miles distant. When I visited during a particularly ferocious heatwave in July 2019, a phalanx of black-robed nuns suddenly appeared bearing water bottles and filed silently into the welcome coolness of the nave, where in rows they prayed and sang. The resulting ambiance possessed a rare beauty and sense of uniqueness, an unforeseen moment of experience that seemed uncannily extended beyond time. After their service the sisters of all ages then dispersed, childlike towards one corner of the church where souvenirs and postcards were for sale. They gathered there like so many blackbirds happily bathing in the dust. On the way back down the hill under the unforgiving sun, I chatted with a few of them and learned they had travelled from a remote monastery in France and the ascent to the cathedral of Sion was the culmination of their journey.

The Last Pilot

I wrote this poem after coming across a brief interview with the last living Battle of Britain pilot on the anniversary of the campaign. When I was young these heroic airborne survivors were legion, dispensing their stories in books and TV programmes. The national myth of the plucky few was ever brazenly reinforced, but as individuals such men always seemed to me to present themselves modestly and to embody values of self-reliance and a noble moral sensibility. Over the last couple of decades these airborne warriors have dropped from the tree with every passing season, this gentleman being the last crisp russet leaf on the branch. Now the tree is bare and we are the poorer.

Death of a Trophy Hunter

This poem relates to an article I read in a national newspaper in 2019 featuring the legally sanctioned yet inherently cruel exploits of the big game trophy hunters who, securing the financial rewards of those who organise this global business continue to indulge their 'sport' with impunity. The article concerned a young American woman who was photographed kneeling with her still warm hunting rifle beside the giant Aslan head of a male lion, smiling into the camera and giving the thumbs up sign.

The Slowing Ride

Drummaids is the name of a hill, a wide sloping expanse on the edge of Epping Forest, where I would play as a child. The derivation of the name has various contenders, but the most romantic is that it began as Drummer's Maid, due to a drummer boy who courted a maid here and, when he did not return from the war, the heartbroken lass took her own life at this spot. This hill formed the centre of a pastoral domain where my developing imagination could freely exercise itself, away from the homestead yet near enough to be connected, an extension of it's security. The grassy hill with its choice of well-trodden paths down which we sledged in winter and trudged back up with our toboggan steeds, where we played hide and seek or 'war' in summer, was our own patch in a greater Epping Forest garden. But one summer's day when I was 11 years old and playing with two friends, an adult male stranger appeared from nowhere and began threatening us. This disturbing episode signalled the end of innocence and when that autumn I entered the forbidding environment of an all-boys secondary school, the close of my childhood.

Rarae Avis

The Hunterian Museum is found on the first floor of the Royal College of Surgeons of England on the south side of Lincoln's Inn in London. In the nineteenth century the museum's curators built on the anatomy and pathology collections of the eighteenth-century anatomist John Hunter. Despite losing part of the collection during the Second World War when the building was damaged by bombs, there today exists an unrivalled assemblage of human and non-human specimens, as well as models, paintings and sculpture. Currently the museum is undergoing renovation and will reopen in late 2021.

Lip Service

This poem came in response to the experience of several funerals, but is principally concerned with that of my friend, the teacher and writer Beatrice Worthing, who died aged 100 in 2015. Beatrice was passionate about Francophone literature and especially the life and poetry of the symbolist era poet Émile Verhaeren, to whom she dedicated her working life. Her detailed biography of the poet, scrupulously researched in Paris and Brussels after the war and completed in the late 1950's has regretfully never been published in its original English, but thankfully was translated into French and published by the distinguished Mercure de France in 1992.

The Guiltless

Margaret Bervoets was a writer in her early twenties residing in Tournai, Belgium, when the Nazis brutally intruded. Unable to bear any form of tyranny, the free-spirited young woman abandoned her job as a popular high school teacher and volunteered for the resistance, for whom she undertook a number of perilous intelligence gathering observance duties. It was on one of these missions that she was detected and arrested, as they attempted to clandestinely photograph an enemy airfield. Condemned by military court she spent the next three years a captive of the Gestapo, incarcerated in prisons across Germany until her brutal execution by guillotine at Wolfenbüttel on August 7th 1944. Her moving final letter is a testament to selflessness and spiritual patriotism.

II

Possession of the Florentine

This poem was inspired by a photograph of a Florentine ivory comb displayed in the Phaidon edition of 'The Civilisation of the Renaissance in Italy' by the legendary art historian Jakob Burckhardt, but it also incorporates memories of similar objects whose intricate carvings and ghostly presence I have long admired on my travels in museums across Europe.

The Final Journey

This poem relates to the period leading up to the final persecution of Vienna's Jews during the Anschluss in March 1938. The title is taken from the first book I read concerning the Holocaust when I was a secondary school pupil in Essex in 1979. At this time the Holocaust was barely mentioned, it was certainly not taught in schools, nor was it present in public awareness in a form that was visible to a child or young person. It was instead an impossibly huge boulder of recent European history waiting to roll over us. I found *The Final Journey* in the school library by chance one lunchtime and was transfixed by its harrowing contents. This sparked what has become a lifetime's ultimately futile search to somehow gain mental purchase on the most industrially realized genocidal event in human history. Yet I have always tried to approach this 'subject' obliquely, by a different route to merely reiterating the horror, which to me seems the only viable option. This poem is an example of that, since it treats the situation of the victims and perpetrators before the final atrocity actually, when the lives of the persecuted are systematically reduced, remoulded and the scope for opportunism by the perpetrators and the inherent humiliations and absurdities drastically augments. Such an environment is a direct communication from history which has an ever more urgent bearing on our own time.

Two Poems after Trakl

These poems take their inspiration from the Austrian poet Georg Trakl and constitute an experiment that lies somewhere in the fought over region between translation and original work. Here, three figures are active, the original poet, the translator and a new voice, the poet who has sneaked in under the folds of the translator's cape, as it were. My idea was to update Trakl to a modern urban setting of decay and disintegration in which I used his characteristic rhythm and structure, and to a degree his language, while at the same time seeding that rich topsoil with something of my own poetry.

Celan in Stuttgart

This poem records some of the events in the final two months of the Romanian-born German language poet Paul Celan, whose writing was heavily influenced by the persecution of the Jews and the murder of his own parents in the Holocaust. In March 1970 Celan travelled from Paris to Stuttgart to read his work at a bicentenary celebration of the German poet Hölderlin. Celan was at the time suffering from a depressive illness and chose to read a number of cryptic verses which appeared to bear no relevance to the poet being celebrated and thus did not go down well with bemused Hölderlin scholars and dignitaries present. On his journey back to the French capital, Celan's mental state was exacerbated when he stopped to visit the famous Crucifixion altarpiece by Matthias Grünewald at the Isenheim Monastery in Colmar which recalled to him the suffering of his parents in a Nazi internment camp. Not long after this, Celan had a traumatic experience on the metro with a friend when a Nazi sympathiser suddenly yelled down the carriage towards them 'Jews to the ovens!!'. Sometime a month later Celan wrote his last poem 'am Sabbath', walked onto the Pont Mirabeau and drowned himself in the Seine.

Three Days

This poem was written after watching the televised 2019 Conservative party conference. But the identity of the political party itself is not the case in point. The well-oiled mechanism of the event, the monotony of sound-bites and slogans of the participants left in their wake an air of delusion and moral failure which struck me as betrayal of humanity, yet one was transfixed by the mediocrity of the outward performance, a nightmare without the concession of wakening.

Charenton

Charles Meryon (1821–1868) was a French artist and one-time sailor who suffered from colour blindness. Working principally in the medium of etching, Meryon became known for his 'eaux-fortes de Paris' during the 1850s and was courted by the poet Baudelaire. His drawings of the medieval city on the brink of change in the 1850s are highly detailed and expertly executed but are suggestive of his encroaching madness. In several of his works fantastical creatures or otherworldly beings make their incongruous entrance, while in others morbid scenes are incorporated. A few years after his etchings had been published Meryon, an increasingly eccentric figure who had long endured poverty and neglect, suffered a mental collapse and was brought to the infamous Charenton lunatic asylum. Seemingly recovered he was released but then readmitted in 1867, dying there the following year.

Last Rose

This poem was inspired by the photograph of a rose by the Czech photographer Joseph Sudek (1896–1976) Sudek, who lost an arm as a soldier in the First World War, was famous for his sublime interior shots, almost always in black and white and exuding a certain reverential silence and melancholy. Many of these were taken in Sudek's tiny primitive studio, whose window onto the courtyard garden acted like a canvas, with Sudek simply recording what he saw passing there over seasons and years. Often his images of passers-by or trees are depicted through misty or rainy window panes. But the artist was equally talented with landscapes, procuring haunting street scenes of a vanishing old Prague and extraordinary monumental images of trees in states of decay located in the Mionsi forest of northern Bohemia.

III

Vanished Spirit of Bruges

As a translator and admirer of Belgian writers and poets I have been a regular visitor to the 'Venice of the North' for two decades. Like its Southern eponym I have been saddened to see the gradual decline in its former authentic atmosphere, which in any case was only clinging on in the older ecclesiastical quarter of the Carmerstraat and surrounds. Mass tourism is unsurprisingly underpinning this degradation, with visitors pushing out further and further into the once undiscovered corners in order to escape 'the snake', what locals term the main tourist procession that moves in an unbroken mass between the Markt, the Dijver, the cathedral and the beguinage. The city burghers in their relentless greed for revenue have ensured no stone is left unturned where further commercial opportunities are concerned. There feels little air left now for the past to breathe and only perhaps in a rare oasis like the Jerusalem church, the café Vlissinghe or along the often deserted quai of the Potterierei can the soul be lightly touched by the breath of what once was.

The Garden of Silence

This walled off garden which does not admit the public is for the benefit of the convent sisters who reside in a Monastery at the centre of the tiny islet Isola San Giulio in the lake of Orta in Piedmont. Tourists are ferried over from the mainland so they can visit the 12th Century basilica and make a circular tour on foot, hopefully and instructively named 'the path of silence' around the base of the monastery enclosure. Abundant signs remind visitors to respect the site and its inhabitants by temporarily adopting the virtue of silence, but these are dispiritingly ignored. The garden however remains inviolable, from here the daily day tripper invaders are strictly repelled and the barely glimpsed sisters alone sequester themselves in its leafy keep.

The Bunkers at Wissant

Along the Côte d'Opale of the Pas de Calais can still be found a good many German bunkers, pill boxes and casemates dating from the war, residues of the main strongpoint of Hitler's Atlantic Wall. One of many large-scale building projects by the Todt organisation, this 1,670 mile coastal defence, the work of thousands of slave labourers, many of whom gave their lives in the process, was the Führer's grandiose fantasy to protect the Reich as a 'Fortress of Europe'. The giant bunkers at Wissant are striking in their situation, having since tipped over and slid down the sandy incline towards a pond or lagoon, so their empty dark embrasures now face the limited stretch of this brackish water rather than the infinite expanse of the sea. Redundant monoliths, their erstwhile function is indistinct to any who were not aware of it and they live now only as immovable shapes or obstacles in the natural landscape.

The Gore

This is the name given to the untamed boulder-strewn shore which signals the end of man-made habitation to the west of Porlock bay in Somerset. From this point there is nothing but unstable cliffs prone to landslides, and between them lost woodlands of scrub oak and stunted silver birch woven with blue grey lichen that occasionally give way to secret coves such as that of Embelle or Glenthorne. Here begins at Porlock Weir the path which following thickly wooded cliffs punctuated by combes leads the walker to isolated Culbone church, in a grove whose environs were once occupied only by lepers and charcoal burners. Coleridge was a visitor, Southey too, they had their evening nook in the Ship Inn at the bottom of Porlock Hill. The landscape between Porlock Weir and Glenthorne is one where human intrusion is necessarily brief and non-destructive and thanks to its inaccessibility, it is, like the coast south of Hartland Point in North Devon, one of the last vestiges of truly wild country in England.

Lost Domain

This lost domain is Ashley Combe, below Exmoor and above the aforementioned Gore, where once a manor house in the Italianate style stood on an escarpment halfway up a steep hill clothed in woodland. The mansion was the country retreat of Lord Byron's daughter Ada Lovelace, the celebrated mathematician and pioneer in the evolution of computing. Ada's engineer husband Lord King planted thousands of exotic trees and created a landscape of faux medieval battlements, tunnels, look outs and follies, held together by interlocking paths and drives. The South West Coast Path runs along the edge of the terrain, even taking advantage of some of the existing tunnels. Ada's 'Ashley' was a phantasmagoria of architectural whimsy, a mesmerizing symbiosis of natural landscape and aesthetically driven artifice. Today all is in an advanced state of decay and abandonment, nature has reclaimed the site almost entirely, but the mysterious atmosphere left by these decaying ruins is palpable.

Acknowledgments

The poems gathered here date from the last four to five years, since the publication of *The Sleepwalkers* in 2016. The exception being the two Trakl-inspired poems which are very much older but which I recently revisited, feeling that the time had perhaps come to foist them on a an even more environmentally ravaged and spiritually degraded world. I should like to thank Robert Selby and *Wild Court* for presenting these, and others collected here. Likewise Patricia McCarthy at *Agenda*, and Hugo Williams at *The Spectator* for publishing a number of these poems in the first instance. I should like to express special thanks to Katie McCrae who did such a wonderful job of editing my voluminous Notes and to my agent Joanna Marston for her tireless labours on behalf of my work. I should also like to thank Deborah Preston for providing the ingenious poem title of 'Lip Service' and Emma Mountcastle for her selfless maintenance of my existential well-being. I am also grateful to those friends, fellow poets and translators who have shared an interest in the progress of this collection and here particularly I should like to acknowledge the contribution of Kathleen Rooney, Richie McCaffery, Pandora Kennedy and Margaret Holroyd.

www.ingramcontent.com/pod-product-compliance
Lightning Source LLC
Chambersburg PA
CBHW020216090426
42734CB00008B/1096